BLACK & DECKER®
HOME IMPROVEMENT LIBRARY™

Deck & Landscape
Ideas

Cy DeCosse Incorporated
Minnetonka, Minnesota

Contents

Library of Congress
Cataloging-in-Publication Data

Deck & Landscape Ideas.
p. cm.—(Black & Decker home
improvement library)
ISBN 0-86573-688-X (hardcover)

1. Landscape gardening. 2. Garden
ornaments and furniture. 3. Decks
(Architecture, Domestic) I. Cy DeCosse
Incorporated. II. Series.
SB473.D425 1996
712--dc20   96-1752
                             CIP

CY DeCOSSE INCORPORATED

A COWLES MAGAZINES COMPANY

Chairman/CEO: Bruce Barnet
Chairman Emeritus: Cy DeCosse
President/COO: Nino Tarantino
Executive V.P./Editor-in-Chief:
 William B. Jones

Created by: The editors of Cy DeCosse
Incorporated, in cooperation with Black
& Decker. ● **BLACK&DECKER** is a trademark
of the Black & Decker Corporation and
is used under license.

Creative Director: William B. Jones
Group Executive Editor: Paul Currie
Associate Creative Director: Tim Himsel
Art Director: John Hermansen
Project Manager: Ron Bygness
*Vice President of Development Planning &
Production:* Jim Bindas
Production Staff: Gary Sandin
Photographer: Bill Lindner
Production Manager: Jim Muñoz

Printed on American paper by:
 R. R. Donnelley & Sons Co. (0496)

Also available from the publisher:
 *Everyday Home Repairs, Decorating
 With Paint & Wallcovering, Carpentry:
 Tools • Shelves • Walls • Doors, Building
 Decks, Kitchen Remodeling, Home Plumbing
 Projects & Repairs, Basic Wiring & Electrical
 Repairs, Workshop Tips & Techniques,
 Advanced Home Wiring, Carpentry:
 Remodeling, Landscape Design &
 Construction, Bathroom Remodeling,
 Built-in Projects for the Home, Refinishing
 & Finishing Wood, Exterior Home Repairs
 & Improvements, Home Masonry Repairs
 & Projects, Building Porches & Patios*

DECK *Ideas*

LEISURE FURNITURE

*Luxury traditional styles for relaxing in comfort outdoors.
A collection of designs to enhance garden, terrace or poolside patio.*

A luxu...

LOUNGER 5090
6' 6" 1980mm
...perbly comfortable
...slated lounger, with
...ulti-position adjustable
back and teak wheels,
enabling you to follow the
sun! Available with full
length mattress, with
headrest.

...d Protect The Natural B...

Pearl Gray

Desert Sand

716 Naturaltone Cedar

Storm Gray

Caramel

Polar Blue

717 Naturaltone Redwood

Ginger

Brick Red

Redwood
9705   9892

Photo courtesy of Milt Charno & Associates

▲ **This multilevel deck** turns a steep, rocky, unusable hillside into an attractive and very usable outdoor living area. The top level can be used for lounging and sunbathing, the middle for dining and socializing, and the lower level doubles as a step leading to the yard.

Photo courtesy of P & M Cedar Products, Inc.

▲ **This large, contemporary deck** has three distinct activity areas: an open, spacious social center, a separate dining area, and space for an elevated hot tub. A low bench defines the angles of the deck and leads the eye to the raised area around the hot tub.

What makes a great deck?

A great deck is an outdoor living area that functions as an extension of your home. It accommodates your family's lifestyle with flexibility for socializing, recreation or relaxation. A great deck turns an ordinary yard into a beautiful showplace.

To inspire you with ideas for creating your perfect deck, we have gathered over 150 stunning color photographs of spectacular deck designs and features and compiled them in *Deck & Landscape Ideas*.

In the first section you will discover how to make the most effective use of your existing space. Many elements included in outdoor living areas are multifunctional. Fences, arbors and trellises add visual interest and help to manage sun, wind and rain. Built-in benches can be used as storage bins, and flower boxes with wide edges double as seating. Style and design ideas for gazebos, benches, steps, railings and flower boxes are shown throughout.

The second part of the book is a portfolio of more than 50 color photographs of fabulous showcase decks. Gorgeous single-level and multilevel designs offer ideas to help you design a deck that suits your family's specific needs.

Whether you are adding a simple platform outside your back door or designing a multilevel masterpiece, this book is full of creative and practical ideas to help you design a great deck.

▲ **Small but elaborate**, *this redwood deck makes efficient use of space by building around an existing tree that provides shade and adds an interesting focal point. An overhead arbor also shelters users from the sun and creates a link between deck and house. Simple wooden benches provide seating and create a boundary for the deck.*

◀ **A simple line** *with an elegant design style is consistent throughout this multilevel redwood deck. Seen in the open railings and flower boxes, these elements help emphasize the various levels that divide the areas of this deck.*

▲ **The basic lines** *and shapes in this deck add visual interest and guide the eye. Contrasting decking patterns emphasize the change in levels between two deck areas.*

PLANNING

Flexibility for many functions

When designing your deck, plan so that "form follows function." First determine what you want to use your deck for, then plan a deck to meet all your family's needs in one attractive form.

Be sure your deck will accommodate a variety of activities including cooking and dining, sunbathing, playing games and entertaining. Also include areas for shade, relaxation and privacy.

Be generous with space and plan your activity areas so that one doesn't interfere with another. Traffic patterns can be controlled by using features like steps, railings and planter boxes to create walkways.

Photo courtesy of Southern Pine Marketing Council

▲ *This deck/walkway* controls the flow of traffic and provides areas for comfortable relaxation. The angled benches with attached planter boxes also create attractive, visual lines.

▼ *The activity alcove* created by combining a raised platform with an overhead arbor provides a shady play area or a quiet, out-of-the-way retreat.

Photo courtesy of Archadeck

▲ *A built-in bench* saves space and supplies seating. The decorative, open-weave pattern of the railings encloses the space but doesn't confine the user.

Photo courtesy of Archadeck

▲ **The angles and shape** of the upper level on this deck are repeated in the contour of the bench on the lower level. The different levels function as distinct activity areas separated by railings, steps and benches.

▲ **A terraced deck** allows users to enjoy the outdoors with an unrestricted view. The dining area is bordered on three sides by a raised level that leads into the house.

Sets of stairs can be sculptural links between levels and activity areas. This wide, open stairway guides traffic from an upper-level dining area to a larger entertaining area on a lower level. The vertical balusters of the railings give the deck a formal look and design continuity throughout. ▶

Photo courtesy of Archadeck ®

▲ **This deck wraps around** the house for easy access from anywhere inside. The shape of the deck, with its curved corners and smooth, continuous line of low benches and flower boxes, complements the shape of the house. A set of wide steps leads from the deck to a ground-level patio.

PLANNING

A smooth transition from indoors to outdoors

A social gathering moves easily from indoors to outdoors when a comfortable deck welcomes you into a lush, open-air living space. To get maximum enjoyment from this natural extension of indoor space, you must consider all elements of your yard, as well as your personal likes and dislikes.

Outdoor rooms are more comfortable when they are divided into several smaller areas. The deck ideas in this book are excellent examples of how to create comfortable, usable living space in almost any outdoor environment.

Both architecturally and aesthetically, the materials, colors and textures used for your deck should complement and harmonize with those in your house and landscape.

An open platform deck snugs up to this house and helps soften the stark transition from the predominantly vertical, angular slope of the house to the horizontal flatness of the yard. The simple design of this platform deck complements the contemporary style of the house. ▶

Photo courtesy of Western Wood Products

▲ *Angled benches* follow the contours of this single-level deck, creating efficient living space from a shallow lawn surrounded by thick trees. The wide bench style provides a visual break between the ground-level deck and the dense foliage.

▼ *A colorful flower garden* frames this simple, two-level platform deck. An L-shaped bench on the outside edge of the top level encloses the area and defines the boundaries of this charming outdoor setting.

▲ *An open, airy platform deck* with tiered stairs rises gradually to the door level. It provides a wide, unobstructed surface with plenty of seating on the wide steps.

▲ *An elegant gazebo* adds a charming, shady sanctuary to an outdoor entertainment area. Built-in benches and flower boxes form an inviting path, leading to the steps of the gazebo.

▲ *This custom design* features a sunken garden as the focal point. A terraced deck/walkway surrounding three sides is combined with a low bench built around the ground level to create a frame for the garden.

▲ *Careful attention to design elements,* like the details in the railings, adds charm to this multilevel, multifunctional deck.

PLANNING

Focus on special features

Gazebos, overhead arbors, vertical trellises, flower boxes, hot tubs and fences are special features that add visual appeal and value to your outdoor living space. Even common deck elements, like steps, benches, and railings can be special features if they feature an unusual design.

▲ *A built-in bench provides plenty of seating without using much space. An attached railing adds a comfortable back for the bench.*

▲ *The hot tub on this deck is surrounded by a raised deck, for seating or sunbathing. A planter box built around an existing tree also provides a shady place to sit.*

13

DESIGN

Simply stated or dramatically detailed

Subtle touches can make the difference in the finished look of a deck. The shape of the deck itself, the decking patterns, and the styling of rails, stairs and other design attributes play a big part in the finished look of your deck and help unite it with your home.

The size of a deck and its surroundings will determine what kinds of design features to include. Small decks in limited spaces should include a limited number of multifunctional elements, like built-in benches that can also be used for storage, or planter boxes and steps that add seating. Large decks should use structural elements like railings, arbors and trellises to break up the space and make it more visually appealing.

Photo courtesy of Weyerhaeuser

▲ ***The herringbone pattern*** *used in an overhead arbor helps diffuse sunlight and casts a textured shadow pattern on the deck below.*

Photo courtesy of Archadeck

▲ ***The contemporary design****, featuring crisp, white vertical railings, gives this deck a fresh, clean look.*

Photo courtesy of Milt Charno & Associates

▲ **The elegance** of this stately home is complemented by the stylish deck design. The simple lines and sleek styles seen in the benches and steps work beautifully to unify the deck, pool and house.

Photo courtesy of Archadeck

Photo courtesy of California Redwood Association

▲ **Open-weave construction** of the overhead arbor adds interesting shadow patterns and reduces the effects of the sun's rays on the deck below. Lattice is also used as an attractive screen to hide an unsightly area underneath the deck.

The rich redwood used in this California deck is one of its most impressive ▶ features. The smooth, curving lines of the benches and railings guide the eye over the wood's elegant beauty to different areas of the deck.

15

DESIGN

Bring a new dimension to your domain

▲ **The natural elements** surrounding this redwood deck help dictate the unique shape of the ground-level platform. The weblike pattern used in the decking and the angles of the railings visually extend the deck between the trees.

▶ **The asymmetrical angles** of the railing are repeated in the built-in bench to give a continuous line that defines the edge of this deck. The wide, low bench also serves as a railing that doesn't obstruct the view.

◀ **A specific theme** can be created by using elements that have a distinct design style. The pagoda design used in these matching arbors gives an oriental flavor to this outdoor space.

▲ **Large three-tiered deck** *creates a comfortable social gathering area on the edge of a sprawling lawn. An open platform style makes it easily accessible. This deck helps to divide this large, grassy space into smaller, more useable areas.*

Design

A well-designed deck uses its environment to create beautiful settings and valuable living space from previously unused land.

▼ **An elaborate overhead** *arbor with a lowered ceiling creates an intimate alcove within the larger deck setting. Steps leading into a sunken area are also used as seating.*

Large spaces are divided into smaller areas that are more comfortable and versatile, either by separating deck areas with design elements, or with multiple levels. Steep slopes and otherwise rough terrain can be transformed into functional living areas by using creative deck designs.

▲ *The **underside*** *of this cantilevered deck is paneled for a rich, finished appearance. The same finished style is carried throughout the entire deck. Contrasting stains are used as a design element.*

▲ *Two **existing trees*** *are incorporated into this unique deck. A striking starburst decking pattern is featured in a raised platform area.*

▼ *This **outdoor area*** *is divided by the distinct angles of the vertical railing. The attractive railing encompasses a dining and entertainment area, then continues around the hot tub setting. A raised platform and overhead arbor provide privacy for hot tub users.*

▲ **The layered design** of the railing, and the flared shape of the steps as they wrap around the hot tub, add visual interest and complement the wood lap siding of the house.

▲ **The staircase** includes a large landing that divides the staircase into balanced areas. The middle landing allows the stairway to follow the contours of the slope.

▶ **The size** of the lower-level platform of this deck is proportional to the larger second level. The shape and angles of the lower-level bench reflect the same shapes and angles seen in the steps and railings around the upper level.

DESIGN

Balance and Proportion

To achieve balance within a deck environment, integrate design elements for a clear, consistent look throughout the deck. When designing an outdoor living area, it is important to create a comfortable relationship between the planes of the intended floor and walls in the open space. The deck area should feel enclosed but not confining. Complete the feeling of balance by keeping all elements in proportion to your house and the other structures in your yard.

Photo courtesy of P & M Cedar Products, Inc.

▲ **The raised deck** that extends from the back was built large enough to balance the expansive size of this house. The rustic design of the house is complemented by the rough, sturdy deck.

Photo courtesy of California Redwood Association

Wide, low steps keep an open feel to this deck even though walls of the house surround it on three sides. The design of the decking, and the shape and size of the deck itself, work to visually hold back the imposing walls and establish a comfortable, open-air room. ▶

SUN/SHADE

Natural climate control for your deck

▲ **Natural shade trees** *are used on this poolside deck to create a cool retreat from the heat of the sun. A flat, open platform located away from the dining area is a perfect place for sunbathing.*

Whether you're a sun worshipper or a shade dweller, a versatile deck offers something for everyone. Overhead arbors are a simple, elegant way to cool off a sunny area on your deck. Vertical trellises and screens also have a charming appeal. Open-weave style arbors and trellises provide shade and allow air circulation through the lattice. To determine placement of these structures, observe the migration of the sun across your deck and note its location at peak-use periods of the day. Take advantage of natural shade givers, such as trees and large bushes. These natural elements can be incorporated as part of your deck design to help control comfort in your outdoor living area.

▶ **A retreat unto itself**, *this raised deck area has a sunny area for hot tub users and a shady dining area sheltered by a large arbor overhead.*

▲ ***Another way*** *to filter out the sun's rays is to use a screen as part of your vertical or overhead structure. A thin, light screen attached to the arbor or trellis lets in plenty of light but keeps the area cool.*

◀ ***The design*** *of the arbor above creates a nice shadow pattern on the floor of this delightful deck. The multilevels provide areas for food preparation, intimate gatherings and sunning.*

◀◀ ***An overhead arbor*** *links the existing trees with the deck and the house and creates a sheltered dining area. The large tree in the center creates shady spots in other areas of the deck.*

23

▲ *The unique design* of this overhead structure creates a comfortable retreat from the heat. It uses widely spaced wooden strips for the roof construction, which allows cooling breezes to circulate through the structure.

SUN/SHADE

There are many attractive and effective options for controlling sun and shade. Trellises, arbors and gazebos offer maximum impact in a minimum amount of space. The charm of an overhead arbor is enhanced by the fascinating shadows cast by the unique shapes and patterns. The perfect spot for relaxation, a graceful gazebo is an interesting focal point for any deck.

▲ *A large, open arbor* provides scattered shade patterns that diffuse the brightness of the sun's light around this poolside deck area.

Photo courtesy of P & M Cedar Products, Inc.

Photo courtesy of Weyerhaeuser

▲ ***The importance of paying attention*** *to design details is evident in the beautiful silhouette of this deck at sunset.*

▲ ***Enjoy the outdoors***, *no matter what the weather. From inside the shelter of a screened porch, you can walk out to either a shady corner of the deck, or an open, sunny area.*

▼ ***A sunny poolside area*** *is surrounded by an elevated observation deck. The shady area under the deck can be used as a comfortable spot to cool off. The upper deck also blocks the heat from the downstairs area inside the house and keeps it cool.*

Photo courtesy of P & M Cedar Products, Inc.

▲ *A **charming waterside gazebo** extends an invitation for intimate dining. This freestanding structure serves as a place to enjoy a warm sunset after supper or as a sheltered retreat from rain and sun.*

GAZEBOS

From Simple to Sophisticated

Gazebos are a great way to add dimension and give an elegant touch to your outdoor living area. In addition to their graceful appearance, multifunctional gazebos increase the versatility of your deck. A gazebo can act as an outdoor den, an alfresco dining area or a private, romantic hot tub setting.

▶ **This gazebo** *has a solid roof and completely screened walls to shelter users from sun, rain and insects.*

▲ **A lattice gazebo roof** *casts interesting shadow patterns. The open-weave design allows a breeze to circulate and the open walls are consistent with the airy look of the roof.*

▲ **This unusual gazebo design** has the feel of a primitive hut. A connected deckway leads to the detached area of the ground-level deck to create a quiet resting area.

◀ **This semi-enclosed, freestanding gazebo** creates a cool, secluded retreat in a shady, wooded area.

▲ **The design detail** of this gazebo gives a formal look to this deck setting. The vertical boards used in the gazebo design create a visual style compatible with the design of the railings.

▲ *A gazebo built over* an extended area of the deck has a solid roof that shelters a hot tub. This roof provides partial seclusion and shelters users from the elements.

◄ *Cedar shingles* and the exaggerated angle and height of the roof give this striking gazebo its unique look. The triangular shape of the roof is echoed in the angle of the tiered steps and the planter boxes.

▲ *The delicate style* of the open walls and lattice roof give these twin gazebos a refined look. Built-in benches provide a comfortable place to sit while viewing sunsets on the water.

GAZEBOS

Today's gazebo can be as elaborate or as simple as you like. Open and airy, with a lattice top and just a hint of wall, or completely enclosed with a solid roof, a gazebo can function as part of the deck itself or on its own as a freestanding retreat within your yard or garden.

▲ *This raised gazebo* creates a more intimate area on this multi-level deck. The intricate pattern on railings of the stairway and the gazebo is an attractive design feature that visually unifies the entire deck.

FENCES, ARBORS & TRELLISES

The framework for fantastic deck design

The thin, straight boards *used to make the alternating pattern of the overhead arbor work well with the rectangular shape of the space. The shape of the trellis sections makes the narrow space seem wider.* ▶

▼ **The unique shape** *of the arbor reflects the shape of the deck area below. The decorative railing with a built-in, angled bench adds an enclosed, intimate feeling to this separate alcove.*

Fences, vertical trellises and overhead arbors are the walls and ceilings of your outdoor room. They help to buffer noise, provide privacy and control the effects of sun and wind in your deck area.

All of these structures play an integral part in the look and feel of your outdoor living space. They add beauty and establish a visual style, and should be designed to complement the related structural and visual elements in your space.

FENCES

Fences are as varied as the materials with which they are built. Choose a fence style appropriate to its planned use.

A recreation area should have an open fence for easy access and low-maintenance plants for minimal care. A fence around a sunbathing area should be tall and solid for privacy.

A fence can also be included strictly for decoration. A well-designed fence should reflect the style of your home and harmonize with the other elements of your outdoor living area.

Because a fence is as much a part of the neighborhood's landscape as your own, it is important to check building codes and neighborhood ordinances if you are including a fence as part of your plan.

Photo courtesy of Archadeck

◀ ***The railing*** *of this steep stairway works like a fence to keep the foliage back from the deck. The shape of the deck below is also defined by the railing around it.*

Photo courtesy of Western Wood Products

▲ ***A tall, solid fence*** *gives privacy to a comfortable sunbathing spot. The construction allows cooling breezes to circulate through the fence.*

Photo courtesy of Western Wood Products

▲ ***You may choose*** *to add partial fences, or a combination of fence and railing, as was done on this deck.*

Photo courtesy of Western Wood Products

▲ *The horizontal pattern* in this fence creates a dramatic look when backlit by the sun. The pattern also is seen in other design elements of the deck.

Photo courtesy of Western Wood Products

▲ *The attractive design pattern* in the railing adds an artistic touch. The intricate detail acts as a screen around the deck area, and the railing serves as a privacy fence.

▶ *Decorative railings* throughout this redwood deck reflect the style of the deck's other structural elements, including built-in benches and overhead trellises. The rail serves as a fence, defining the deck's boundaries. The intricate pattern can be seen winding in and out of the surrounding foliage and around the perimeter of this spacious deck.

Photo courtesy of California Redwood Assoc.

ARBORS & TRELLISES

There are a variety of styles and designs available for arbor and trellis structures. Most are made of an open-weave lattice construction that can be as intricate or simple as you like. The result is an airy structure that provides a feeling of enclosure and privacy while allowing you to enjoy the view. Arbors and trellises can also be used to support climbing plants or to camouflage unsightly objects like air conditioners, pool pumps or utility poles. An arbor or trellis is an attractive way to create a frame around a view or highlight a focal point of your deck area.

Photo courtesy of Western Wood Products

▼ *The thick beams, rounded edges and intricate latticework on this overhead arbor give a formal appearance to the dining area of this poolside deck. Outdoor lights also have been installed for nighttime use.*

Photo courtesy of California Redwood Assoc.

◀ ***This arbor supports and frames*** *an attractive hanging swing, creating a comfortable place to relax and unwind.*

▲ ***The elaborate layered design*** *of this arbor includes a lowered false ceiling made of lattice material. The deck area underneath descends into an enclosed, sunken gathering area. The combination of the overhead structure and the sunken sitting area creates a private, secluded niche on this deck.*

34

Photo courtesy of Western Wood Products

Photo courtesy of Archadeck

▲ *A small but charming* arbor with attached overhead trellis dresses up this simple garden bench.

▲ *The thin boards* and perpendicular design give this trellis an oriental look. The open design complements the other structural elements and provides a place for climbing plants to grow.

Photo courtesy of California Redwood Association

◄ *A vertical lattice panel* provides privacy for deck users and conceals the shower area from the deck.

Photo courtesy of Weyerhauser

▲ *Add a finished touch* to an ordinary deck. The lattice around the bottom covers the unsightly underside of the deck and creates a hidden storage space.

Modest use of built-in accessories creates a large, open level on this redwood deck. A flower box built around a tree has been included in the deck design. The plain benches make effective use of space and are designed to match the clean, straight line of railings.

ACCESSORIES

The Elements That Make the Difference

The accessories you use to decorate your "outdoor room" should be as multifunctional as the deck design itself. They should allow you to use your deck comfortably and conveniently in a variety of ways.

Be sure to provide places for people to sit and lounge. Benches, steps and planter boxes with wide edges provide ample seating without taking up too much space. Cooking and dining areas should include countertops and serving tables. You can also furnish your deck with customized accessories, like a built-in barbecue, fire pit or hot tub.

▶ **This deck's built-in flower box** *sits alongside the raised platform of the deck, adds interest as well as extra seating.*

Benches

▲ **Designed for optimum** use, these benches have seats on both sides. Built-in triangle-shaped flower boxes add an interesting angle.

▲ **Sturdy, wide built-in benches** follow the lines of this octagonal platform, which also includes an overhead arbor to create a shady play area.

▲ **This angled niche** is a cozy alcove—perfect for reading or relaxing.

Flower Boxes

▲ **A contemporary rectangular** shape used on the flower box and other structures on this deck creates continuity.

▲ **Benches and built-in flower boxes** form a rectangle and create a charming courtyard within a larger deck area. The flower boxes at the corners break the long benches into smaller, more comfortable, sections.

▲ **Flower boxes** built into the platform levels form a diagonal line leading up the steps.

▲ Custom-built flower boxes are incorporated into deck design; they are built as part of the bench structure, as one combined unit.

Miscellaneous

◀ **Simple lines** *and shallow, terraced steps provide a place to set house plants during warm weather.*

▲ ***A built-in fire pit*** *creates a warm, cozy gathering spot on this narrow, sheltered portion of the deck. Large pillows add a splash of color and offer casual, comfortable seating.*

Accessories

▲ *A dramatic doorway* within this outdoor living space is created when fence and arbor come together. The stylish design used in the framework on the fence panels ties into the overhead arbor and a solid pitched roof, sheltering an adjacent area.

◀ *The furniture accessories* on this deck have a handsome design style that matches the sturdy lines of the railings and other built-in deck accessories.

▲ **Bench and deck** *are built around an existing tree. The wraparound bench protects the tree and creates a shady sitting area or tabletop.*

▶ **A special alcove** *along the walkway of this deck houses a grill, keeping it out of the traffic area.*

A PORTFOLIO OF DECK IDEAS

GROUND-LEVEL DECKS

A level-headed way to handle an awkward angle

A basic, single-level deck built close to the ground can be the solution to many problems found in an outdoor environment. Narrow spaces, awkward angles and soggy ground areas are just some of the obstacles a ground-level deck can help overcome.

Whether it is attached to the house or standing alone in a far corner of the yard, a ground-level deck adds an interesting focal point to a flat, open space. Ground-level decks can be tailored to fit any size or shape, which makes them the perfect solution for filling irregular or oddly shaped areas of a yard.

An island of outdoor enjoyment, this freestanding redwood deck is an elegant place to enjoy a number of outdoor activities. A hot tub serves as the focal point of the deck. Built-in benches provide seating for socializing. An attractively tiled counter and sink area, with storage space underneath, can be used for food preparation. The lattice screen allows a gentle breeze to flow through, yet gives deck users a sense of privacy. The attractive latticework also adds an appealing backdrop, which frames the entire outdoor area.

GROUND LEVEL

The layout of a ground-level deck should allow easy, one-step access to and from the house. Single-level decks are often close enough to the ground that they don't need railings, although in many cases railings are still included to define boundaries and give a sense of unity to the deck setting. The ground-level decks shown here have a spacious open feeling that makes them an ideal place for sunning or entertaining.

This ground-level deck has two open sunny spots for users to enjoy. The wide step creates an easy transition from the spacious upper level to the lawn below. ▶

▼ *Two auxiliary deck areas,* one with a flat, wide bench built around the edge and one with room for a table and chairs, extend from a smaller upper landing area outside a patio door. The upper area is a convenient grilling spot and has an area for storing extra chairs.

Photo courtesy of Western Wood Products Association

Photo courtesy of Milt Charno & Associates

▲ *A **large single-level deck** is detailed with a complex contemporary railing and flower box designs. The open expanse of the single-level deck is balanced by the large, two-story modern home.*

▲ *The **distinctive shape** of this single-level deck is enhanced with built-in planter boxes and benches. The rounded corners and decking design detail give this deck a smooth, finished line.*

▲ **This deck makes** *effective use of a shallow space. A wide, low bench follows shape of the deck.*

◀ **This two-tier, platform** *deck offers an unobstructed view. The use of terraced steps allows a smooth transition from deck to yard.*

GROUND-LEVEL DECKS

Photo courtesy of Georgia-Pacific Corporation

▲ *The flower box/bench* combination is an intelligent and beautiful use of space on this raised deck. A deckway leads to a flat platform used for sunbathing.

Photo courtesy of Archadeck

▲ *A single-level deck* with simple lines surrounds this brick patio. The stain used on the deck matches the color of the patio brick, giving a unified look to the entire outdoor area.

GROUND LEVEL

▲ *An entire backyard is converted into an outdoor deck area. This eliminates yard maintenance and enables the designer to incorporate more elements into the design. A diagonal style of decking design adds interest and accentuates the fire pit. This outdoor living area also includes a gazebo and a separate dining area. A high privacy fence along the edge of the deck way provides a backdrop for the entire outdoor setting.*

Photo opposite page courtesy of Western Wood Products

Photo courtesy of California Redwood Association

◀ *Four terraced levels* with *built-in flower boxes make up this spacious open deck. The second step down is wide enough to serve as an alternate activity area. The top area is open and bright and has a privacy fence for secluded backyard sunbathing.*

▼ *The monotony of a large, level grassy area is interrupted by a deck featuring flat, stacked levels, with clean lines and a rigid geometric design. Steps lead down to the ground level, and an arbor above a built-in corner bench provides shelter.*

TERRACED DECKS

A tiered or terraced deck is made of two or more platforms combined to create a stacked effect. A terraced deck is particularly effective in a yard with a gradual slope, where the individual tiers become gracefully decending steps. The separate tiers also can be used to define separate seating, dining and play areas—turning unusable terrain into functional outdoor living space.

Photo courtesy of Western Wood Products

GROUND-LEVEL DECKS

A graceful transition from the deck to the ground

▲ *Slightly raised above the ground,* this single-level deck is at the same level as the interior floor of the house. French doors swing open to combine this roomy outdoor living area with the interior living space. A built-in bench, close to the grill, doubles as a handy table and defines a cooking and eating area.

▲ **An elegant redwood deck** *was built into a slope and around an existing tree to create this dramatic outdoor space. An overhead arbor extends from the house across a portion of the deck, creating an enclosed, private dining area with a spectacular view. The existing tree also serves as a screen between the area under the arbor and the casual seating area at the corner.*

▼ **This single-level deck** *rests on a pedestal that extends up to meet the connecting terraced stairway. The unique pedestal base creates a circular cantilever that leaves a lot of open room underneath.*

RAISED AND MULTILEVEL DECKS

Elevated decks may rise just inches off the ground or many feet in the air. They are usually designed to extend out over a steep hillside or from a second-story patio door. Raised decks can solve the problem of a severely sloping yard by extending over and above the hard-to-reach space. High-rise decks are often elevated far enough above the ground to allow an unrestricted, sweeping view of the surroundings. The space beneath a raised deck can be used to create a cool, shaded sanctuary or it can be completely enclosed and used for storage.

▼ *Built on a drastic incline, this expansive bi-level deck sits high on stilts. A stairway leads down the steep incline to a landing that opens onto the deck area. As the stairway continues down the slope, the deck juts out from the steep hill, over the water. A spectacular, versatile deck area now takes the place of a rocky, unusable slope.*

Photo courtesy of P & M Cedar Products, Inc.

▲ *The top platform* of this raised deck is elevated to floor level where sliding doors provide access from a large family room. The unusual, layered design of the railings along the steps is also used in the sleek lines of the benches on the lower level.

Photo opposite page courtesy of Blakesee-Lane, courtesy of P & M Cedar Products

Photo courtesy of Milt Charno & Associates

◄ *This enclosed, raised deck* sits upon a beautifully finished pedestal angled at the bottom to help manage a slope in the terrain.

Photo courtesy of Milt Charno & Associates

▲ **The raised levels** of this deck descend in a layered design, creating four separate decks linked by shallow steps. The highest level is a cantilevered deck that extends out over the lawn.

▶ **A modest deck** is adorned with a delightful overhead arbor and a bright, sunny sitting area. Wide, open steps lead down to the lawn. Lattice screen adds a decorative touch to the bottom of the deck and covers the unsightly area under the deck.

Photo courtesy of Weyerhaeuser

Raised Decks

Photo courtesy of California Redwood Association

▲ ***An elaborate raised*** *redwood deck accommodates many activities. A screened-in porch keeps out the insects; an open area on the upper level is perfect for sunning. A comfortable deckway becomes another activity level as needed.*

Photo courtesy of Southern Pine Marketing Council

▲ ***Three tiered steps*** *lead to the top level of this raised deck. The open platform on top creates a spacious area for playing or just relaxing and enjoying the view.*

Photo courtesy of Archadeck

▲ ***The steps*** *from the raised level lead down to a secluded patio and seating area. The built-in bench on the lower level mirrors the angled lines of the raised level.*

A steep slope is made into usable living area by adding an elevated deck. Existing trees are left as interesting features of the deck's surrounding scenery. ▶

▼ *This raised deck* offers a fantastic view that looks out to a scenic lake. It is private, secluded among the treetops.

Raised levels take decks up to the wide-open spaces

▼ **The sweeping splendor** of this raised deck is surrounded by a spectacular view. The simple lines of this elegant redwood deck are enhanced by a curved railing — all that's needed to add a touch of class to this natural beauty.

▲ **This large multilevel redwood deck** *sprawls down a steep hill and divides into four separate use areas with small landings between the levels. An attractive alternative to the rough terrain below the deck.*

MULTILEVEL DECKS

Dividing your deck into various levels is one way to make it multifunctional. Each level serves as an individual activity area. Wide, open stairways link the levels.

The multilevel masterpieces shown on this page make the most of their sites. A steep slope, a rocky terrain and a shallow, flat expanse are transformed into outdoor living areas that are wonderfully effective, multifunctional favorites.

▲ **This expansive home** has several different deck areas extending from different rooms inside the house. The use of different levels gives each deck privacy from the others. The ground area under raised decks can also be utilized.

▲ **This deck integrates with a natural stone retaining wall** as it curves down this rocky slope. As the deck winds down the hill, different levels extend out over the steep incline. The bottom steps have a set of benches on either side of a small landing. The overgrown retaining wall behind creates a small, intimate sitting area.

▲ **Two large levels** *of this multilevel deck are joined by a stairway. The lower level has a table and benches for dining and entertaining. The upper level is spacious and sunny–a perfect spot for sunbathing or for a child's play area.*

▲ **This raised deck** *is built above a rocky lakeshore. Wide steps from the main deck area descend to the beach. An octagonal area of the deck, used for casual dining, is two steps down and surrounded by a railing.*

▲ **An expansive two-level deck** *extends from both stories of this house with access to the deck from many different areas inside the home. A portion of the upper level is fully screened, making this area of the deck more useable. Lattice covers the area under the deck and creates a hidden storage space.*

▲ **Delicate white lattice** is used as a design feature throughout this appealing deck. Entertain on the upper level; the lower level has a hot tub surrounded by lattice panels for privacy. The lower platform provides an area for sunning and relaxing. An overhead arbor designates a separate dining area.

Photo courtesy of Archadeck

▲ **This deck design** *makes efficient use of the area under the raised deck. The space is finished and used as a secluded place to gather with the family or quietly relax alone.*

Multilevel Decks

Make the Most of Places with Limited Spaces

▶ **The different levels** *used in this impressive addition dramatically increase the amount of usable space. The food preparation area is located on the upper level, high above and away from the dining area below. Angled stairways, with sizeable landings at each turn, link the two spaces and provide small activity areas or resting places. An attractive support column underneath the raised portion of the deck doubles as a small storage closet.*

Photo courtesy of Milt Charno & Associates

Photos on both pages courtesy of Archadeck

MULTILEVEL DECKS

◀ **This multilevel deck** makes efficient use of a steep
hillside that leads to a lakeshore. The upper deck
includes an area with an overhead roof that looks out
over the steep slope to the dining area on the lower level.
To enjoy a scenic view of the lakeshore while dining,
the lower deck area is built over the lake.

▶ **A second level** is built almost directly above the
ground level to give the two areas of this deck privacy
from one another. The two levels make access from
inside the house much easier. A stairway leads from one
level to the other.

▼ **The three levels** of this deck are connected by
spiraling staircases. The angles of the deck itself are
repeated in the railings and built-in benches.

Photo courtesy of Archadeck

RECREATIONAL DECKS
Pools & Hot Tubs

Including a pool or hot tub in your outdoor living area will provide hours of fun and relaxation for your family and friends. And an outdoor pool or hot tub area is made more functional and more attractive when surrounded by a deck. The seating area around a hot tub serves many functions. Raised benches can be used for sunning, and for housing the plumbing and storing deck accessories and tools. Poolside decks need to accommodate poolside activities. They should include ample space for sunbathing and entertaining. Wooden deck surfaces drain well and create safe walkways for swimmers. Frame your poolside area with a deck to create an open, sunny spot for sunbathers.

◀ *This rooftop deck area is surrounded by a screen fence that provides privacy for hot tub users. The hot tub is enclosed by a small deck that can be used as a shelf ledge for plants or towels, or for seating in and around the hot tub. The screen shelters the deck from wind and sun but still lets through a comfortable breeze.*

Hot Tubs

▲ **The deck area** that holds this octagonal hot tub overlooks a large pool area below. A railing with a built-in planter box/bench combination gives some seclusion to the hot tub area and a wide bench for sitting or lounging is built around the sunken hot tub.

▶ **A corner of this deck** juts out to create a rounded alcove with a sunken hot tub. The separate area gives hot tub users a sense of seclusion.

▲ *A smooth, wide built-in bench* defines the hot tub area of this deck. An enclosed tub sits on one level and butts into the next level to allow access to the tub from two different levels. The smaller upper area can be used for sunning or lounging. The spacious lower level can accommodate more people. A level above the hot tub is used for cooking and is easily accessible from the house.

▲ *The lower level* of this deck area consists of large hot tub enclosed by a wood rail and an overhead arbor. Steps lead to a second or main-level walk-out deck extending from the house.

71

RECREATIONAL

Pools

Great for sunning and entertaining, a deck is the perfect architectural element for any poolside setting. It is important to provide a shaded area for protection from the sun. It should be roomy enough to accommodate sunbathers and outdoor furniture comfortably. Wooden poolside decking is always more comfortable to walk on because it does not get as hot as other materials.

Photo courtesy of Milt Charno & Associates

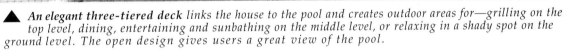

▲ *An elegant three-tiered deck* links the house to the pool and creates outdoor areas for—grilling on the top level, dining, entertaining and sunbathing on the middle level, or relaxing in a shady spot on the ground level. The open design gives users a great view of the pool.

◄ *The terraced steps* of this redwood deck wrap around an above-ground pool to give the pool a built-in feeling. They are wide enough to be used for seating or sunbathing. Sun worshippers can follow the sun as it moves down the winding steps from the upper deck level overlooking the pool.

Photo courtesy of P & M Cedar Products, Inc.

Photo courtesy of Archadeck

▲ **A large raised deck** *makes efficient use of the yard by creating more outdoor living space without sacrificing usable lawn area. The existing lawn under the raised deck is intact and usable. A large landing breaks the imposing stairway into two manageable sections.*

Photo courtesy of P & M Cedar Products, Inc.

◀ *Detailed decking patterns and intricate step angles beautifully frame this hot tub setting. The high wall behind the hot tub and the angle of the tub to the house and deck create a cozy private niche for tub users. The gorgeous wood grain is seen in built-in amenities throughout the deck.*

▲ **Two spacious levels** on this contemporary deck offer plenty of room for outdoor entertaining. A hot tub located on a roomy upper level has elevated privacy yet allows users a dramatic view. Below is a larger deck area with built-in benches and plenty of space for sunbathers.

RECREATIONAL

▶ **This efficient**, freestanding redwood deck has it all: a raised, sunny area for a hot tub, and a comfortable, shady dining area with an elegant arbor overhead. The attractive design links this activity area with the brick patio.

Photo courtesy of California Redwood Association

RECREATIONAL
Pools

▲ **An elegant poolside space** *includes an alfresco dining area separated from the redwood poolside deck by a slight elevation. A classic design style is used in the white wrought-iron fence and the planter and patio furniture.*

▲ **This contemporary deck** *uses black accents in the furniture and trim around the pool to contrast with the light wood in the decking and the blue colors of the water.*

▲ **A hot tub** *located in a sunny corner of this deck is the focal point for deck users. This featured area is surrounded by plenty of space for dining and entertaining, with wide built-in steps leading down to an open lawn.*

▲ *An attractive wooden decking* is cooler and safer than other materials used around pools. An open-weave lattice doubles as a decorative privacy screen and windbreak.

▲ *This raised deck* completely surrounds a ground-level pool. The deck is flush with the main level of the house. A screened-in outdoor room adds comfort from the elements, while a flat, open lawn allows you to enjoy the yard in pleasant weather.

DINING

Enjoy Eating Alfresco

A deck used for outdoor dining or cooking should be easily accessible from the kitchen. An outdoor cooking center should provide enough room to comfortably prepare food close to the grill. Tables, whether built-in or moveable, should be located conveniently close to the food preparation area, yet out of the range of blowing smoke.

▲ **An enclosed gazebo** surrounds a built-in hot tub area that looks down onto another level of the deck, used for dining and
socializing. These two separate areas are each sheltered by an overhead structure. All areas of this multipurpose deck are linked
▼ by decorative railings and connecting deckways.

◄ **An outdoor dining area** is enhanced by the attractive curves in this built-in table. The curved design follows the custom curves in the
deck. A contrasting decking pattern is used in the steps decending from the top level. A curved bench built around an existing tree adds
extra seating options.

DINING

Each distinct deck area should be the same size or slightly larger than an indoor room with the same function. An outdoor dining area should be approximately the same size as an indoor dining room. Be sure to allow for the fact that outdoor furniture often is larger than conventional indoor furniture.

Photo courtesy of Archadeck

Photo courtesy of Southern Pine Marketing Council

▲ *Enjoy comfortable dining in any weather. A screened room connects to the deck area and gives the feeling of being outdoors.*

▲ **This outdoor dining area** offers users a view of an attractive enclosed hot tub alcove and other points of interest. The dining area has plenty of space for outdoor furniture and also includes built-in benches for additional seating.

▲ **This outdoor dining area** is located close to the patio doors for easy access from inside the house. The deck area includes plenty of open space for larger social gatherings.

▼ **A small deck** with two separate areas capitalizes on efficient use of space. The design was kept simple to eliminate clutter and keep space as large as possible. Detail in railing is the only design element used.

▲ **Wide benches** around the outside
edges of this deck accent the unusual
shape and provide a comfortable spot
for lounging in the sun.

◀ **The designated dining area** on this
large deck is easy to get to from inside
the house and all areas of the deck. The
casual dining atmosphere offers a view of
the hot tub setting, which is enclosed by a
raised deck and an overhead arbor. The
grid pattern used in the decorative railing
adds an art deco style to the design and
also serves as a partial privacy screen.

▲ *Colorful flowers* surround this very functional two-level deck. A patio door opens to lower level for easy access from the house. A raised level has plenty of room for social gatherings. A built-in bench with an interesting angle serves as a railing on the edge of the elevated deck and provides additional seating, if needed.

Entertaining

Entertaining on your deck is easy and comfortable with amenities that accommodate your guests. Save space by including structures that provide extra seating. Many bench styles and step designs can be used as comfortable seating.

Photo courtesy of Georgia-Pacific Corporation

▼ *Enjoy a meal,* and the view, under a shady umbrella on this pleasant deck. Built around a pool, this deck has plenty of room for sunbathers and pool users alike. Built-in benches along back fence provide additional seating for social gatherings.

Photo courtesy of Archadeck

MULTIPLE USES FOR YOUR DECK

The Freedom of Being Functional

A great deck is one that can accommodate many outdoor activities at one time. Careful planning and an eye for detail will give you a deck that can be used for any occasion or desired activity. Plan so that traffic flows easily from inside the home to each section of your outdoor area, and make use of amenities that perform more than one function.

▶ *This **multifunctional deck** includes an area for sunbathing, a hot tub area, an area for casual dining and a social gathering space. These activity areas are far enough apart to be used independently, or they can be integrated and used as one outdoor area.*

Photo courtesy of Archadeck

▲ *An expansive, stylish redwood deck* has two spacious levels with plenty of room for large gatherings. A poolside level is open and sunny with amenities for sunbathing and outdoor dining. A lower level, three steps down, becomes a cozy spot for intimate gatherings. Wide steps lead from the lower level down through the middle of a natural stone retaining wall.

MULTIPLE-USE DECKS
Include All the Angles

Photo courtesy of P & M Cedar Products, Inc.

◀ **This functional deck** was designed for multiple uses. One area includes an attractive hot tub setting with a raised deck built around the tub and stylish design details used in the railings and stairways. A second dining area is conveniently located within easy access of the house and barbecue. As an attractive and functional built-in feature, a long bench follows the edge of the ground level and doubles as a railing.

Photo courtesy of Archadeck

▲ **A lower-level courtyard** is one small part of this multiple-use deck. This shady, quiet area is surrounded by colorful flowers. The interesting triangle-shaped flower boxes add a point of interest and separate the long, connected benches.

89

Multiple Uses
Multifunctional Favorites

▼ ***This expansive deck*** *includes two or three large areas, each with multiple uses. A raised deck in back, a sunken courtyard area to the right of the terraced area, and a large dining area on the top level of the deck can each function as a separate activity area. All areas can also be united to form one multifunctional area for large social gatherings.*

Both photos courtesy of Archadeck

▲ **Higher level** *overlooks a lovely courtyard, built around a large shade tree. The terraced steps have a built-in combination bench/flower box that also sets off the courtyard.*

Photo courtesy of Western Wood Products Association

▲ *A hard-to-maintain, narrow space* is now a multifunctional deck way that can be used for a number of activities. A fire pit surrounded by a diamond-style decking pattern is the center of one area. The diagonal direction of the decking pattern leads to an open dining area.

Photo courtesy of California Redwood Association

◄ *This spectacular redwood deck* is divided into intimate and cozy corners. One distinct alcove includes a sunken dining area located under an elaborate gazebo. The existing trees have been integrated as design elements.

MULTIPLE USES

▶ *A modest ground-level deck* *can be used effectively in a small space. A sunny hot tub area invites sun worshippers to enjoy the deck, while shade lovers can enjoy the natural beauty on a comfortable shaded bench.*

◀ *Even small outdoor areas* *can be multifunctional. In this open, sunny deck area a solid fence creates privacy for sunbathers, a secure area for children to play or a secluded spot for dining and entertaining.*

▼ *A separate cantilevered deck* area
extends this portion of the deck out over
a steep slope, creating a scenic overlook. The
remaining deck area is spacious and usable
for many outdoor activities. A short, wide
box structure built around a tree becomes
a built-in bench.

◀ *An open deck area around a pool is a hot spot for sun worshippers. The attractive lattice provides privacy while a refreshing breeze flows through the open weave. The simple lines of the decking pattern complement the intricate detail of the latticework.*

▶ *The simple lines of this small deck have a multi-functional appeal. The terraced steps double as seating or can be used to hold plants and other decorative deck embellishments. The open design offers a sunny place to relax with a clear view from the top. Even a modest deck can increase the value of your outdoor living space.*

Multifunctional

▲ **The deck area around this hot tub**, with the addition of built-in benches, was designed to save space. A raised deck built around the tub gives it its own small alcove for privacy. The hot tub area is connected to, and is easily accessible from, other levels and activity areas of this deck.

LANDSCAPE *Ideas*

WHAT MAKES GREAT LANDSCAPING?

Great landscaping is a work of art. Think of your yard as a picture that is created using aspects of design, such as line, form and color, in the same way an artist uses them. The picture your landscape creates is a reflection of who you are and what you like. We have included over 140 color photographs of great landscaping designs in *Deck & Landscape Ideas* to help you plan a landscape that fits your taste and needs.

Landscaping can serve many functions, such as helping to control sunlight, wind or a sloped yard that may be eroding. A newly built home that is bare of grass or trees offers the chance to create a landscape exactly the way you want. With careful planning, you can create an outdoor space that is beautiful and

functional. You can use landscaping to create additional living space outdoors or to provide privacy for your existing outdoor space. A beautifully landscaped yard increases the value of your property by enhancing the attractiveness of your home and making it more inviting.

Deck & Landscape Ideas will help you create a landscape that is ideally suited to you and your yard. We begin by helping you determine your landscape needs and what type of yard you have. You will also need to know the budget you are working with. To help you design your personal landscape, this book includes a portfolio of photographs of beautifully landscaped yards. Here you will find ideas for patios, porches, decks, walkways, trees, shrubs, plants, enclosures and lighting to inspire you and help you plan a landscape design that best fulfills your specific requirements. There are even ideas for dealing with special landscaping needs, such as water, climate and unusual or unusable space in your yard.

You don't need to be an expert to create a beautiful and satisfying yard. Whether you do the work yourself or hire someone to do it for you, you will still need to spend time planning if you want your landscape to serve specific functions. This book will help you design a landscape that will allow you to enjoy the fruits of your labor for years to come.

This photo and opposite page (top) courtesy of Bachman's Landscaping Service. Sue Hartley, photography.

Photo courtesy of Dundee Nursery

PLANNING

Before you begin landscaping, you need to plan the project. This includes deciding not only what type of yard you want to have, but how much money you can spend. You must take into consideration the area you are living in: who are your neighbors and what are their yards like? You will be making choices, not only about design, but about types of materials and how much they cost. If you want to include more elaborate features, you might have to scale back in one area in order to emphasize another that is more important to you. Working these decisions out in the beginning will help you avoid problems later on in the project, saving time and expense. Landscaping your yard is a fun and exciting project that needs time for preparation but also lets you create the yard you've always wanted.

Photo courtesy of Bachman's Landscaping Service. Sue Hartley, photography.

DETERMINING YOUR NEEDS

What kind of landscaping design suits your personal needs and style? If you have a growing family, you will probably want to include a playground and maybe empty yard space for active games. If you are an avid gardener, you will want your yard to include areas for growing flowers or vegetables. Perhaps you have always wanted a yard with exotic features, such as a fountain or a small gazebo. This is the time to consider your favorite outdoor environments and how you might recreate them in your own yard.

DETERMINING YOUR NEEDS

Budget

Budget is your first determining factor in landscape design. A small budget will of course limit the extent of your design, but not the ability to create interesting areas within your yard. Be prepared to purchase materials such as wood, stone and/or brick as well as plants such as trees, shrubs and/or flowers. Some of the structures you might be building include fences, decks, trellises and patios; you will also want to consider planters, walkways and steps. Researching the cost of materials before you begin the actual work will help you make sure your plans fit your budget.

Carefully considering your taste and needs as well as your existing yard space will eliminate problems in the future and give you a head start in designing the best landscape possible. Note the difference in expense but not in resulting styles in the following photos.

A brick walkway lined with shade-loving plants leads to a tranquil hot tub enclosure. The materials used to build this enclosure were not particularly expensive, but special design elements like the windows shown here can add to your costs.

This suburban home has a young, fairly inexpensive landscape. A cluster of small shrubs and a young tree are featured on one side of the front walk. Brilliant red salvia provides balance and color on the other side of the walk. These plants will continue to grow and fill this space. Adding a few new plantings each year is an inexpensive way to continue to increase the value of your landscape.

Round concrete pavers with a unique texture were used to create a pathway that leads from one area of the yard to another. Small, inexpensive elements like these pavers are a great way to add an interesting visual accent to your landscape at a reasonable cost.

DETERMINING YOUR NEEDS

Size & Contour of Your Yard

Determining your needs includes looking realistically at the yard space available to you. Is it small or large, square or unusually shaped? What are the natural elements you have to contend with? Does it have many trees? Consider how large they are and how old. Note which parts of your yard receive the most sun and from which direction. Be prepared to work with your yard and not against it. You can turn unusual features into points of interest and divide a basic square yard into unique shapes with distinctive lines and characteristics.

Natural elements are used to define the boundaries of this rolling, open lawn. The open grass area can be used for outdoor activities or large gatherings. Neatly landscaped areas help define the boundaries of the yard, yet still maintain the feeling of wide-open spaces. Tall, well-shaped evergreens and several smaller bushes create a border at the back of the yard and give the space some privacy.

Retaining walls can create usable space in areas that would otherwise remain unused. This wall provides large planting areas for bushes, flowering plants and even a small tree. The interlocking blocks complement the brickwork of the house and help to unify the landscape.

This photo and all on opposite page courtesy of Bachman's Landscaping Service. Sue Hartley, photography.

A large house and accompanying yard demand an equally large landscape. Here several varieties of tall trees have been planted in strategic places within the landscape. The large trees balance the size of the structure and soften its sharp angles. Flowers in front of the house add color and elegance.

The stately elegance of this house is reflected in the graceful landscape that surrounds it. Well-manicured hedges combine with benches to frame small beds of white impatiens. Their crisp square angles are also reflected in the open, square design of the deck and the way it frames the neatly trimmed grass. The expansive rolling lawn helps to balance the house and serves as a natural extension of the deck area.

Photo courtesy of Dundee Nursery

DETERMINING YOUR NEEDS

Private Space

You will also need to consider factors such as your desire for privacy. City dwellers find privacy in short commodity and often long for an enclosed, secluded area with obvious boundaries. Fencing is the obvious choice for creating these private areas, and the amount of privacy desired will determine what type of fencing is used. Landscapes that don't have such a demand for privacy might include less enclosed structures like open-walled gazebos, arbors and trellises. Refer to local codes when building landscape structures for specifics such as legal fence heights, required setbacks from property lines and other code issues. For safety reasons, consult with local utility companies before you start any outdoor construction.

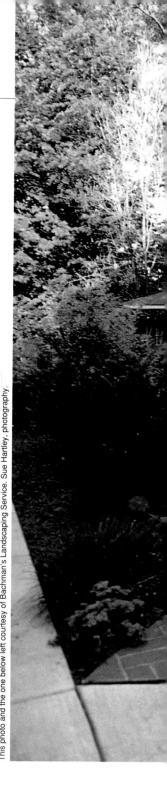

This photo and the one below left courtesy of Bachman's Landscaping Service. Sue Hartley, photography.

Photo courtesy of Terry Tempus, TCT Landscaping.

A solid brick-and-wood fence gives character and privacy to this quiet setting. The brick adds interest to the fence and coordinates with the stone pavers and small boulders and stones bordering the pond.

A private area was created by building terraced retaining walls into a steep slope. The wooden retaining walls provide a place for vertical flower gardens and planting beds.

Lush green trees and shrubs create a beautiful, living visual boundary and give this open patio area some needed privacy. With a living privacy fence, however, your privacy may be diminished when the leaves fall.

DETERMINING YOUR NEEDS

Function of Your Yard

As you begin the process of designing your yard, consider your favorite activities and personal taste. If you love to entertain, you might want to include patio space large enough for parties and lots of outdoor lights for nighttime events. If you wish for solitude, you can create private corners shaded from the rest of the yard or interesting walkways that lead to unexpected areas. Nature lovers might wish for a yard that replicates the freedom of the country and has lots of room for wildflowers and wildlife.

Even if your yard is small, you can create miniature environments that provide a sense of your own style and satisfy your needs. If your time is limited, you might want to design a yard that requires little maintenance but still allows you to enjoy the outdoors. Terraces, fences and other structures add interesting lines and textures to a landscape while serving a practical purpose.

Large beds of multicolored impatiens lead the way to a swimming pool tucked away on a wooded hill. Lush greenery surrounding the pool creates a smooth transition from pool to yard and gives pool users a scenic landscape to enjoy.

An impressive tulip bed creates a sea of red, white, yellow and pink that brightens the house and fills the yard with color in early spring. Later, when the bulbs are finished blooming, flowering annuals will be planted among the bulbs to continue the colorful theme throughout the season.

A separate niche was created in this deck with built-in benches and integrated flower boxes. Colorful annuals overflow from the planters to frame this intimate alcove.

113

DESIGNING YOUR YARD

Designing your yard is fun and exciting. This is where you actually put your plans and ideas on paper. It is a good idea to draw your yard as it is now, including the house and any other features that will be retained or are important, such as where the sun hits, where the neighbors are located and what the view is from particular areas. Include trouble spots, such as eroded slopes, areas that receive little rain and places where noise or litter are a problem. Take a walk around the neighborhood, noting which yards appeal to you and any elements they contain that you would like to include in your own design.

When designing your yard, remember to leave lots of room around plants for future growth. Draw any structures you would like to include, noting the types of material they will be made from and size and location relative to other areas of the yard, in order to maintain a balanced and integrated look.

DESIGNING YOUR YARD

Materials

Stone, masonry and wood are primary building materials for landscape construction. Stone and masonry give your landscape structures a feeling of permanence. Wood has a natural, warm look, is easy to shape and can be painted or stained to match existing structures.

Whenever possible, choose landscape materials that either match or complement the materials already used on your home. For example, if you have a brick home, a patio made from similar brick will be more appealing than a poured concrete slab. Or, if you have a Tudor-style house with exposed beams, a retaining wall built from rough timbers is more appropriate than a wall built from interlocking concrete blocks.

Man-made stone products cast from concrete are a good choice for landscape structures, considering the increasing price and dwindling supplies of forest timber and natural stone. Interlocking concrete block, brick pavers and other manufactured stone products are widely available, easy to install and very durable.

If you prefer the look of natural stone, try to select a type of rock that is common to your geographic region. Local stone makes your landscape look natural, and it is much less expensive than stone that must be shipped long distances.

Interlocking block (below) is made from molded concrete that is split to provide a rough face resembling natural stone. Available in several colors and sizes, interlocking block is used for both straight and curved retaining walls, terraces and raised planting beds. Interlocking block walls create bold geometric patterns.

Concrete block is available in plain or decorative types. This durable building material is used often for free-standing garden walls. The hard, plain look of a concrete block wall can be softened with climbing plants or a surface application of stucco or stone veneer.

Poured concrete is durable and less expensive than other paving products. Although concrete is plain in appearance, it is easy to maintain, making it a popular choice for walkways, patios, walls and steps.

Interlocking pavers *made from molded concrete are used in patios, walkways and driveways. Available in a variety of colors and shapes, interlocking pavers are a good way to add distinctive patterns to a landscape.*

Brick *is an elegant, traditional building material made from molded, oven-dried clay. Available in many styles, brick is used to build patios, walkways, edging and free-standing garden walls.*

Terra cotta and adobe *are molded clay products that are dried in the sun. They are used for patios, walkways and garden walls. These products have a porous surface that can be damaged by water, so terra cotta and adobe are best suited for very dry climates.*

Concrete pavers *are made from poured concrete and are available in many decorative shapes, textures and colors. Inexpensive and easy to install, concrete pavers are used for patios, walkways and steps.*

Crushed gravel

Smooth river gravel

Cut stone (granite)

Flagstone

Glacial rubble stone

Accent rock (quartz blend)

Natural Stone

Gravel comes in two forms: rough gravel made by crushing larger rocks, and smooth gravel usually dredged from rivers. Gravel is sorted by size, and has many landscape uses. Applied as a loose layer, gravel makes an informal, easy-to-maintain pathway. Laid in large beds, gravel lends a relaxed feeling to a landscape while providing texture and color.

Cut stone, sometimes called ashlar, is natural stone that has been cut into cubic shapes. Marble, hard limestone, and granite (shown here) are popular for cut stone. Cut stone is used for both mortared or unmortared walls, patios or walkways. It is an expensive, top-quality building material that gives landscape structures an elegant, timeless appearance.

Flagstone is uncut sedimentary stone that has naturally flat surfaces. Limestone, slate, and shale are common types of flagstone. Flagstone works well with large, expansive landscapes, and is used for walkways, patios, and steps. It is a durable, but expensive, paving material.

Rubble stone is any type of irregular, uncut rock collected from fields, gullies, or stream beds. It can include boulders, glacial debris, rough pieces of quartz or granite, random pieces of limestone or sandstone, or even volcanic rock. Rubble stone often is used in garden walls and retaining walls, and works best in informal, rustic landscapes. Rubble stone is cheaper than cut stone.

Accent rock is distinctive natural stone used as a decoration rather than as a building material. Large, colorful rocks can be partially buried in a planting area or lawn to add visual interest. Accent rocks can range from small 20-lb. pieces to enormous boulders weighing more than a ton.

Wood

Wood and bark chips are used for loose fill on soft pathways or as a ground cover for planting areas. Wood and bark chips are inexpensive and lend a relaxed, casual look to a landscape.

Pressure-treated pine contains pesticides and wood preservatives to make it last. Less expensive than cedar and redwood, pressure-treated pine is used to build fences, retaining walls, raised planting beds, and garden steps. Most pressure-treated pine is green when new, but gradually weathers to a neutral gray. Or, it can be stained to resemble redwood or cedar. In some areas, treated pine is also available in a dark-brown color.

Cedar is a soft wood with a rough texture. It has natural resistance to decay and insect damage, and is used for fences, trellises, and arbors. Use cedar in above-ground structures only: where wood will be in contact with the ground, use pressure-treated lumber instead.

Redwood is a smooth-grained wood with a natural resistance to insects and decay. It is used for above-ground structures, like fences, trellises, and overhead arbors. Avoid using redwood where a structure will be in contact with the ground: for these applications, use pressure-treated wood instead. Because of high demand and dwindling supplies, redwood is becoming more expensive.

Redwood bark chips

Pressure-treated pine

Wood chips

Cedar

Redwood

DESIGNING YOUR YARD

Composition & Color

Composition is an aspect of landscaping that includes the use of scale, line, color and material as well as elements such as focal points and sun versus shade. Consider the composition of your yard as you study your design. Is it balanced? Is color attractively placed throughout the landscape or is it limited to one area? Have you selected flowers and shrubs with varying blooming periods so you have constant color throughout the season? Do the objects you have included complement each other in size and texture, or do they clash? Repetition of color, shape and texture helps to unify a landscape and give your yard a well-groomed, elegant look.

A narrow path of flagstone winds through a large bed of hostas. The large, elegant leaves of the hosta plants create a lush, green ground cover. Some hostas produce decorative spikes of flowers during blooming season, enhancing the landscape even more.

A curved gray retaining wall made of interlocking block creates a flower bed brimming with brilliant color. Bright yellow and pink mums line the front of the bed, while taller yellow calla lilies and ornamental grass create a colorful backdrop. Flowering salvia fills the rest of the bed with deep purple.

A small fountain adds movement and sound to this garden pond. Natural stones, ferns, grasses and waterlilies surround this pond to create a tranquil woodland setting and make it the focal point of the landscape.

121

DESIGNING YOUR YARD

Personal Style

Keeping in mind the importance of what has been previously discussed, remember that landscaping is a personal choice, reflecting your own taste and sense of style. Choose colors and textures that are pleasing to you and a design that fits your nature. Some people will prefer large splashes of color while others will want their yard to reflect more subtle hues. Some will choose the rough texture of stone rather than concrete's smoother surface. An orderly landscape says something very different from one that is more "natural."

Include features in your yard that reflect your individuality. You don't have to rely on the "experts" to design a great landscape. Your landscape will be your own work of art and, above all else, should provide personal satisfaction for years to come.

This photo and opposite page (bottom) courtesy of Bachman's Landscaping Service. Sue Hartley, photography.

The curved line of the rock-filled planting bed creates a soft edge as it meets the neatly trimmed lawn and gives a smooth, rolling feel to the entire landscape. The round edges of the bed reflect the round design used in the gazebo structure seen in the background. And the pink tint in the rock will match the blossoms of the crabapple tree.

To preserve the natural look of this setting, simple wood planks are used as a bridge over a small stream. This thick growth of trees, shrubs, grasses and ferns creates a lush woodland retreat.

Photo courtesy of Terry Tempus, TCT Landscaping

Meticulously manicured European Privet hedges give symmetry and balance to this formal garden. The uniformly shaped hedges encompass flower beds filled with orderly rows of white impatiens. The white blossoms tie in with the white benches and birdbaths, and reinforce the pristine look of this stately landscape.

A multitude of flowering hostas and impatiens create a border of rich color in this shady area. A second variety of hosta planted around a tree introduces a new color while maintaining the overall theme of hostas and impatiens. Hostas are available in both green and variegated varieties.

A PORTFOLIO
of Landscaping Ideas

PATIOS & PORCHES

Patios and porches are outdoor rooms that are an extension of your house. They can be used for dining, entertaining or relaxing, and often act as a transition area between house and garden or other parts of the lawn. A terrace is a patio that is raised above the level of your main outdoor area and is used mainly when dealing with a sloped yard. The elevation of a terrace means it is visually prominent, so keep this in mind if you are planning to build one.

Materials used most often when building a porch or patio are wood, interlocking block, concrete block or poured concrete, bricks made from either terra cotta or adobe (made from molded clay and dried in the sun) and either concrete or interlocking pavers. Each of these materials provides a distinctive pattern and texture. When choosing your materials, remember that they should match or complement your home. Some are more expensive than others, and some adapt more easily to certain construction designs (poured concrete is more easily adapted to a curved area than other types of materials).

This ground-level deck with smooth, curved edges has low, wide-tiered steps leading to a patio level. Wooden benches and flower boxes filled with colorful annuals decorate the open deck and create a cozy outdoor sitting area. Raised garden beds are incorporated into this deck to provide more space for planting.

Brick, a traditional outdoor building material, sets a simple pattern for this modest patio. Brightly colored zinnias and petunias and a variety of green plants provide color as they separate the patio from the rest of the landscape.

A brick patio extends the living area of the home to the outdoors. A small raised deck that steps down to the patio provides the transition from indoor living area to the outdoor living area of the patio. Stately birch trees provide shade, yet keep the space bright and breezy.

This brick patio is a combination seating area and walkway. The curved lines in the brickwork create a smooth visual flow around the rounded planting areas. The planting beds are filled with a combination of flowering bushes, like the potentilla with white flowers; ground-spreading conifers, like the spreading juniper; and more delicate trees, like the birch, with its small limbs and white bark. A solid wood fence gives this backyard patio seclusion and privacy.

Varying the color of the brick in this patio makes it more casual and more visually interesting. The warm color of the brick is set off by white lawn furniture and colorful annuals. Small planting areas are incorporated into the design and filled with shrubs and flowers to brighten and soften this patio setting.

DECKS

Decks are a perfect way to expand your living space to the outdoors. They can either be connected to the house or built free-standing. The design you choose will depend on how you will be using it: for family get-togethers, a place to relax outdoors, a private area for sunbathing or even neighborhood dances. Often it includes a pool or hot tub. If you plan to entertain frequently, your deck should connect conveniently to the kitchen.

Photo courtesy of Bachman's Landscaping Service. Sue Hartley, photography.

This elaborate deck is surrounded by a steeply tiered retaining wall made of the same material as the deck. The main area provides lots of comfortable space that can be used for a variety of occasions. Built-in benches and a large planting box filled with colorful annuals define the edge of the single-level deck. The expansive retaining wall is planted with shrubs and flowering plants that will cover it with lush, living color when mature.

When this redwood deck is viewed from above, lush greenery fills the eye and a sense of undisturbed privacy emanates from below. This large deck features two separate areas, one section of which is built off a sunroom. A large wall made of planter boxes and built-in benches provides seclusion and privacy. The deck extends along the house and one step up leads to the second, more open area bordered by a low wall with built-in planter boxes.

Here another multilevel deck, with many angles, creates a variety of different effects. While the first level is essentially a step to the next, the second level sports a square firepit and is surrounded by matching planters. A small level leads up to the top area which is used for dining. A gazebo built at one end provides shade and privacy.

Unusual curves give a distinctive air to this cantilevered redwood deck which was built on a slope over a wooded area. Nestled among the treetops, this redwood deck is large enough to hold a small table and two chairs on one side and a redwood bench with pillows for additional comfort on the other. Overhead, leafy trees form a sheltering canopy.

An elegant white rail fence defines the lines of this deck as it angles out from the house and down to the yard. The clean, crisp look of the rail matches the design of the house and creates a theme that extends to the neatly manicured landscape.

This multilevel deck is built above level ground to accommodate a sunken firepit that is built into the lower level. The angles and lines of the decking pattern accent the square shape of the firepit. Bushes, flowering plants and ferns, planted in the yard, emerge around the edges of the deck to add color and greenery and to fill the space between the ground and the deck.

133

RETAINING WALLS

Retaining walls are generally used to manage slopes that limit usable outdoor space and also create an erosion problem. Effectively dealing with the problem of erosion, they are also visually pleasing, giving them a dual purpose. Hillsides make it difficult to plant and mow grass or raise other shrubs, plants and flowers. Terraces, two or more retaining walls used for the same slope, have flat areas between them, providing additional growing space, and are useful for slopes that are especially steep.

Materials used for retaining walls are interlocking blocks, stones and timber in a variety of styles. These materials add color, shape and texture to a yard and are sturdy enough to support the weight they must bear. The type of material you choose will depend on finances as well as on the amount of time you wish to invest in your yard. Timbers are easily placed on top of each other and held together with spikes, while stones and interlocking blocks need to be carefully aligned and are generally more expensive.

This handsome retaining wall, made of interlocking blocks, adds shape and texture to the yard. The raised flower beds provide color and are safe from damage caused by traffic or active use of the yard.

Rubble stones and large boulders are used for this retaining wall, which has been built to manage a slope at the perimeter of the yard. Enough flat space has been left between the wall and the fence to plant several trees and shrubs, while flowers and ground cover have been tucked into niches between the stones.

These photos and opposite page (top) courtesy of Bachman's Landscaping Service. Sue Hartley, photography.

This close-up of a rubble stone retaining wall shows how ground cover, artistically planted, can soften the stones' rough edges and provide bursts of color that stand out against the gray, rough texture of the stone.

Here a steep slope has been managed by building high timber retaining walls. Matching timber steps extend from the wall and lead up to the top of the slope. Small shrubs and flowering bushes are planted along the wall and on top of one level. When mature, these plants will cover and soften the angles and edges of this expansive retaining wall.

This retaining wall is built of rounded timbers and has been attractively draped with creeping ground cover. The deep green of the ground cover helps the wall to blend harmoniously with the wooded landscape behind it.

Photo courtesy of Dundee Nursery

Here another steep slope is transformed into a beautiful background for an outdoor deck area by building several terraced walls that have been planted with lush greenery. At the bottom of the wall a built-in bench helps make the transition to the deck area. A large built-in planting box overflows with colorful annuals. The fence at the top provides safety while distinctly separating the lawn from the rest of the space.

This timber retaining wall peeks out between the mature hosta and spirea plants surrounding it. The plants and trees have created an appealing still life that uses the wall as its background. Rocks, large and small, provide extra texture and break up the blend of greenery.

This small, curved retaining wall highlights the two trees it encircles. Pink impatiens and purple salvia fill the empty space around the trees with soft color. The wall provides a distinctive landscaping element by adding interesting shape and texture to the area.

STEPS & WALKWAYS

Steps are used for ascending a sloped yard and need to be level and easy to climb. Walkways are like "hallways" leading from one yard area or "room" to another. They help to direct traffic and are often an extension of steps. While steps are usually built from flagstone, brick, timbers, concrete block or poured concrete, walkways can be made from loose materials, such as rock or bark, for areas with light traffic flow, or from stone, brick or poured concrete for more heavily trafficked areas.

Curved walkways give a softened look to a landscape, while sharp lines and angles fit well with contemporary styles. The shape and type of material you use for your steps and / or walkway should complement both your house and the rest of your yard. Keep in mind color, texture and line when designing this part of your landscape.

Circular stones (left) make a small walkway across a pebbled bed leading from grass to a stone path. The curves add a unique shape to this landscape, providing a point of interest.

This curving walkway (right) is made of brick surrounded by beds of stone and small shrubs. The end of the path turns into matching brick steps leading down a slope. Wooden steps above connect the house to the path.

Red brick steps lead from the sidewalk to the top of this small hill and the house behind it. The bricks match those in the house and add interesting texture and color, making them the focal point in this landscape. Matching bright red geraniums in planters stand on either side of the steps.

These angular steps, although not all the same length, are unified by their similarity in depth and material. Wooden edging connects the different shapes while the various lines themselves work together to create sharp definition and interesting corners.

142

Here a steep slope has been managed with wooden steps leading through rock retaining walls. The two textures, wood and rock, go well with each other and with the surrounding landscape of trees, ferns, bushes and wood chips covering the ground.

This curved walkway extends from the driveway to the front door and is lined with red brick to match the house and garage. A variety of annuals, shrubs and trees border the walkway, while gravel is used to fill in the beds. The overall effect is neat and symmetrical without appearing artificial.

143

Rough flagstone, unevenly shaped, fits well with this landscape's rustic appearance. Hosta plants border the stone, softening its edges, while cedar chips provide color and weed control. Although the effect looks natural and unplanned, much thought and care has gone into creating this path.

This flagstone path wanders directly among the flowers, allowing visitors to enjoy close contact with the garden.

Here, a meandering path bordered by rocks leads through thick woods, beckoning the curious to stroll softly along its leaf-strewn curves.

BEDS & BORDERS

Beds and borders are most often seen lining the edges within and around your property line. They are built up against houses, fences, sidewalks and walkways as well as around trees. Usually outlined with stone, brick or wood, borders create a definite boundary between the bed and the rest of the yard. Used not only to fill in empty space next to structures, they effectively control erosion and act as an accent to the rest of the yard.

Borders can be filled with any number and variety of plants, from flowers to small shrubs and trees artistically arranged to provide a pleasant blend of color and shape. Small rocks or gravel generally fill in gaps between plants and flowers, although some beds simply contain a large mass of flowers that display a riot of color when in full bloom. When creating a border, think of color and contrast, such as light and dark. Location of flower beds is especially important. Research the amount of sun and type of climate plants and flowers do best in before you plant to save expense and heartache later.

This terrace has been built in four levels, creating a staggered border that ends at the house. Neatly filled with small rocks in the same neutral color as the wall, the beds have been planted with mums and several varieties of shrubs and small bushes spaced well apart from each other to give them plenty of growing room.

This photo and opposite page courtesy of Bachman's Landscaping Service. Sue Hartley, photography.

Here a roughly built wall of large field stones creates an attractively casual border for this bed of bright red impatiens.

Vertical landscape timbers curve around this raised bed of annuals and small shrubs, providing a definite boundary between the bed and the walk. A lattice panel behind the border provides an interesting background for the setting and a sense of privacy.

Photo courtesy of Southern Pine Council

A high, terraced retaining wall borders this yard and has been planted with bushes now displaying their brilliant red and yellow fall colors.

This curved gray retaining wall is set off well by the deep green grass below it and the purple, pink and yellow flowers above.

Red tulips and bright purple hyacinths border this walk, showing their springtime colors and brightening the landscape after winter's duller grays and browns. Bricks line the walk in front, creating a boundary between the flowers and the path.

Solid-colored beds of impatiens and a variety of shrubs, including juniper and flowering spirea, border this sidewalk and soften its edges. They provide color and contrast, not only among themselves, but with the rough textures of stone and brick that make up the walkway.

This neat border extends out from around the base of the tree. Filled with wood chips, flowering hostas and daylilies, it creates a soft bed with a quiet and restful appeal.

PLANTERS

Planters are containers in which flowers or smaller plants are grown. They take up much less space than beds, and are attractive because of their distinct shapes as well as their contents. They can be tall or short, of almost any shape and are made from any number of materials, from wood to ceramic. A whole variety of flowers can be grown in planters, where they are often easier to raise. Trailers are a favorite for containers because they hang down over the sides, softening the edges and creating an elegant look. An added benefit of planters is their movability, allowing a change in location either to create diversity in the landscape or to benefit the plant itself.

This square white wooden planter contains a tree rose in full bloom. In cooler climates, container-grown roses need to be treated as annuals.

Wooden planters filled with bright begonias line this walk at intervals, creating a blend of textures and colorful red accents that contrast nicely with the subtler tones around them.

These three wooden planters (above), are really tiers, one built up from the other, and line a matching wooden walkway leading up to a small gazebo. Again, as planters they break up the design of the walkway and are filled with ornamental trees and brightly colored flowers serving as accents to the rest of the landscape.

These built-in planters, filled with begonias and azaleas, line a wooden deck, while smaller flowerpots, easily moved to allow flexibility within the landscape, have been placed alongside them.

153

GARDENS

For many people, gardens are the spice of life. Whether you have been an avid gardener for years or are just beginning to dabble in the dirt, gardens allow you to bask in the outdoors while enjoying creative fulfillment and the beauty of nature at its best. Both vegetable and flower gardens require work, but even when small in scale, their produce is well worth whatever time and effort was expended on its behalf.

Be judicious in your choice of flowers when planning a flower garden; too many can be overwhelming and will compete against each other for soil and sun. Plant smaller flowers in front and larger ones in back, creating rows that complement each other and blend well together. It is fun to plant with the seasons in mind, so that you have a continual show of flowers for as long as possible. Bulbs such as tulips, daffodils and crocuses start a garden in early spring, while primroses and daisies flower during the summer months and gentians and wintergreen come into bloom in early fall.

Gardens are more than just the flowers, fruits and vegetables they produce. Design, color, layout and even structures need to be considered for a pleasing and productive end result. Notice the different plants, their layout and the use of structures in the gardens that follow.

Annuals, flowers that must be planted anew each year, and perennials, flowers that come back year after year, make up this varied flower bed. Annuals grow faster than perennials and are perfect for large flower beds, flower arrangements and planters and hanging baskets.

This elegant formal garden carries an English flavor with its hedges and neat paths. Clipped close, the hedges make up the garden's basic structure while flowers and birdbaths offset their long, green lines. A stone wall surrounds the garden itself, adding another texture and matching the even lines of the hedges to continue the garden's English theme.

Rose gardens are often considered the height of both beauty and gardening ability, as can be seen with this small section of roses. Here a birdbath rests in the middle of an array of rose bushes while a flagstone path wanders among them, broadening the garden's use and allowing closer contact with its flowers.

156

An artful trellis supports climbing roses, a myriad of petunias and rose bushes surrounding its base. The unique design of the trellis goes well with the jumble of color below; together the two create a beautiful and original garden scene.

Beds of tulips and yellow daffodils grace this garden in early spring. The first flowers to emerge after a long and cold winter, they promise that warmer days will follow.

157

TREES & SHRUBS

Trees and shrubs are useful in landscapes for many reasons. They provide shelter and shade, protect the soil, serve as windbreaks and create physical barriers that act as screens, preventing unwanted traffic and controlling noise. They also provide beauty and are a valuable contribution to the conservation of our planet.

When choosing trees and/or shrubs for your landscape, you must first of all be aware of the different kinds of trees (conifer, deciduous, evergreen and palm) and which grow best in your climate. Walk around the neighborhood noting different types of trees in the yards around you, and visit a local nursery to discuss which types of trees are best suited to your locale. A good nursery can also tell you which trees are hardiest and where and how they should be planted.

When you have determined how many and what kind of trees you want, put your plan on paper. Draw a rough design that includes each tree, noting wind direction and amount of available sun throughout the day as well as spacing between trees and other areas of the landscape. Trees and shrubs are an important and expensive investment in your landscape and should be chosen and planted with care.

These shrubs, bushes and trees have been planted to create contrast in the landscape by careful use of differing textures, shapes, sizes and colors. Use contrast selectively: too many contrasting elements produce a landscape that looks random and unplanned.

Photo courtesy of Bachman's Landscaping Service. Sue Hartley, photography.

Planting a sapling is an investment in the future of the planet and generations to come. When planting a young tree, remember that it will grow, so leave enough open space to accommodate its growth pattern. You can balance a young tree with larger landscaping elements, as can be seen here with the shrubs and retaining wall built behind this young tree.

This graceful stand of white birch screens the side of a house, providing shade and privacy as well as beauty.

All photos this page and opposite page (top) courtesy of Bachman's Landscaping Service. Sue Hartley, photography.

These shrubs and small bushes have been carefully planted well apart from each other, acknowledging future growth. Rocks fill in the gaps between them while a long row of hosta lines the tree behind, adding greenery and depth to the overall landscape.

Here a small hedge curves around a stand of bushes, acting both as a barrier and a border. Trees and shrubs can contrast with each other as well as with materials, providing a multitude of textures, colors and shapes.

Hedges make effective barriers without a loss of openness or airflow. Taller hedges protect privacy while providing greenery. Low hedges allow communication with areas beyond your yard. Hedges need to be trimmed and shaped at regular intervals if they are to remain attractive.

VINES & GROUND COVER

Vines are used in conjunction with walls or screens to ensure privacy; mask unsightly fences; soften the hard lines of a fence, wall or house; or simply as additional climbing plants with a trellis or arbor for support. Generally fast growers, they are perfect as temporary screens or even as longer-lasting additions to the landscape. Vines come in several varieties, many of them flowering, that are worth investigating. Some people claim that no garden is complete without them.

Ground cover is used to cover large areas, often under a tree or along a fence or retaining wall. It is also used, alone or in conjunction with other flowers or plants, to shield an unsightly area. Thickly planted, it can help reduce and even prevent soil erosion on a steep hill. It is also used to soften hard edges, fill in gaps between plants or structures and reduce maintenance in hard-to-reach areas.

Here, cinquefoil covers the base of a retaining wall and is beginning to climb into the crevices between the rocks, filling in the empty spaces with its tiny green leaves and adding color and softness to the scene.

Spreading juniper is a ground-hugging evergreen with prickly needles that is a favorite choice for ground cover. Here it spreads across small rocks on a rise leading up from a retaining wall.

Both photos this page courtesy of Bachman's Landscaping Service. Sue Hartley, photography.

Vines are often most striking in the fall, as the flaming red leaves of this ivy show. The contrast between the ivy leaves and the white brick walls of the house is sharp. Keep windows free of vines for an unobstructed view.

Climbing vines need the support of a trellis or similar structure if they are to thrive. Once established, vines require little maintenance although some vines need winter protection in cold climates. Cascading down from flower boxes atop the trellis, flourishing morning glories bear colorful flowers that open each morning with the sun.

163

FENCES, WALLS & GATES

Fences and walls are used to enclose a yard either partially or completely in order to provide definition, security and privacy. They are an effective barrier to unpleasant sights and sounds, and act as a deterrent to trespassers of all ages and sizes. They also block strong winds and unpleasant weather.

Depending on their height and the type of material used for construction, fences and walls send a message to others about what lies within. High, solid walls keep people from peering inside and offer a great deal of privacy. Low or partial walls make your property visible while still serving as a boundary, thus allowing others to enjoy your landscape without intruding.

Fences and walls should integrate with the rest of your landscape, including the house. They also need to be compatible with the neighborhood, so note these types of structures in the yards around you. They can be made from brick, stone or various types and styles of wood, as well as from a row of plants or even trees planted closely together. Stone walls store heat from the sun during the day and radiate it back at night, which makes them ideal for heat-loving plants. Screens and latticework let in light and air, maintaining a connection with the rest of the environment as they create enclosures. Certain areas limit how high you are allowed to build your fence, so check zoning codes before beginning construction.

Gates are a necessary part of fences and walls, serving as a point of entry and exit. They can either blend in with the rest of the fence, in which case they should be of the same or similar material and color, or they can be distinctive and clearly defined. Bright colors and additional trim, such as arches or vines, are ways to heighten a gate and make it an individual part of the wall.

A small trellis above the doorway, made from the same redwood as the fence, sets off this simple iron gate, making this point of entry noticeable and inviting. The gate's open grillwork relieves the severe nature of the fence and provides a pleasant connection between the interior and the exterior of the yard.

165

Here a small picket fence acts more as a border than a barrier, announcing the edge of the yard without fuss. Flowers and climbing plants go well with the fence, creating a small-town atmosphere and a sense of summer's ease.

Latticework tops this high fence, softening its impenetrable face and adding a touch of elegance to a barrier that is clearly not to be crossed.

A wooden fence lines this pool, providing privacy for swimmers and sunbathers inside. Pools can be dangerous to unsupervised children and animals, so the fence becomes a safety feature as well.

167

This low stone wall forms an attractive boundary between two distinct areas within the landscape, separating them without blocking the view. Pink mums at the base of the wall add color and soften the stone's harsher lines.

A low retaining wall made of limestone divides a sloped yard into two different areas. Plantings along both sides of the wall help to blend it naturally into the landscape.

This wall, made of decorative cement blocks in an attractive pattern and with a pleasantly rough texture, serves as a solid, well-built boundary around the edge of the yard.

These three sections of fencing, set several feet apart, are the focal point in this landscape, providing definition as well as artistic style.

TRELLISES, ARBORS & GAZEBOS

Trellises, arbors and gazebos are structures that add extra interest to your yard, especially when covered with vines or climbing plants. A trellis is a lightweight frame of latticework used specifically to support climbing plants; an arbor is simply a bower or open canopy covered with plants and used to provide shade. When built next to the house, an arbor is useful as a transition area and also serves to screen sun and wind. A gazebo is a permanent structure reminiscent of a tiny house with one or more open sides. It can serve as a dining area, a protected sitting space or a private retreat.

Structures such as these are wonderful additions to the landscape but need to be considered carefully. Usually made out of wood, they should blend with the rest of the yard, as well as the house. Scale them appropriately or they'll take over the landscape. A small arbor covered with wisteria or a gazebo tucked among the trees can be enchanting.

Teakwood Garden Furniture by Barlow Tyrie

Shade filters down on benches beneath this arbor while the vines surrounding it provide additional protection and privacy. This arbor cunningly rests on trellises, with the entire structure built as one piece and providing a pleasant seating area.

The beauty of this arbor (left) lies in the design and redwood used for its construction; plants would only hide its character. Covering a walkway, the arbor is a ceiling, screening the sun and weather.

Vines drop down between the slats (below), while sunlight and shade create contrasting patterns, as seen from the underside of this intricately constructed arbor.

A white trellis supports morning glories that fill a wide planter built on top, doubling as a barrier or wall with slats. Impatiens fill a stone bed that borders the trellis, the two features working well together both structurally and as flower beds.

The unique designs of these unusually constructed trellises and arbors are heightened by the elegance of climbing vines. One offers a novel seating area and the other serves as a point of entry into a mysterious garden.

Sporting a tiered and pointed roof, this redwood gazebo is open on all sides, extending an invitation to rest in its shade. Vines and plants surround the gazebo, acting as living walls and enclosing the area in cool, green growth.

Looking like a small house with open windows, a shingled roof, potted geraniums in the doorway and exterior lights to point the way in the dark, this gazebo could come from a fairytale, like a candy house in the woods.

This gazebo features 2 ×2 wood-framed sides made of treated Southern Pine that act as screens, providing a buffer against the weather and shade from the sun. This gazebo acts like a small summer house with four sides and a door; the open walls let in the breeze and sweet smells of summer.

LIGHTING

The purpose of lighting in your landscape is twofold; first, to illuminate, and second, to serve as a safety feature. In addition, lighting adds an artistic touch. Whether by choosing unique fixtures or by illuminating far corners on a dark and rainy night, using light in your landscape adds an element of mystery, magic and romance.

As with other areas you will consider when landscaping, it is important to plan your use of lighting before installing it, and this plan should be based on your overall design. Note areas where unattractive and harsh light already exists and see if you can replace it with something softer. Consider highlighting an attractive feature, such as a certain plant, statue or fountain.

If safety is an important issue, a bright light in your yard will deter intruders. Colored lights around the deck add a festive element to outdoor entertainment.

Walk around your yard at night and note areas that already receive light, whether from the street or a neighbor's house. Imagine how light, strategically placed, would change the effect and add to your existing vision. It is also important to consider where you will be installing lights and burying lines. Make certain your plans conform to local codes.

Light surrounds this multilevel deck as twilight darkens the sky. Fixtures have been placed at intervals along the tiers and encircle the main area of the deck itself, not only providing an accent to the night, but offering security.

Photo courtesy of Bachman's Landscaping Service. Sue Hartley, photography.

Sunlight gives this fountain a pale sparkle during the day while the same water at night, lit from within, takes on a surreal glow. Various fixtures around the walkway and within and without the house work together with the fountain to illuminate the entire area.

Both photos this page and opposite page (bottom) courtesy of Bachman's Landscaping Service. Sue Hartley, photography.

Standing at attention like sentinels, these various fixtures guard their posts, casting light along the path to show the way.

Two large lamps set on pillars across from each other spread their light over the front of this house, brightening the landscape and highlighting the red of the bricks in the walk and the flowers alongside it. Extra light on the ground and the garage add to the expanse of light that covers the area.

This photo and photo at bottom left courtesy of Bachman's Landscaping Service. Sue Hartley, photography.

Here a tree stands illuminated by ground-level lamps while shadows from the corner wall near which it is planted bounce off the wood and run along the rocks.

This small Chinese light fixture looks like an unusual sculpture, creating a focal point in the landscape during the day and providing light at night.

Snapdragons, marigolds and impatiens are lit by this small light in front, their colors looking all the more brilliant in the gleam.

This curved, weathered flower fixture, complete with bent leaves, blends with a bed of irises while, opposite, a whimsical mushroom light adds a humorous touch to the landscape.

A small square light (above), set off by a peaked roof, looks like a house filled with tiny glass windows.

An iron hanging lamp (left), spreads its glow against a brick background.

181

SPECIAL FEATURES

Water, Ponds & Pools

Water can be used as an accent, as with a small pond or stream, or for activity, as with a swimming pool. Both the sight and the sound of water add an attractive element to a landscape. A still pool of water reflecting shadows from a passing cloud or a babbling brook skipping lightly over rocks create distinctly different impressions that should work with whatever other elements make up the landscape. A spray of water adds sound and activity, as does a bubbling fountain. Even a bird bath brings life to the simplest of landscapes.

Plants should highlight your use of water, but not detract from it. Depending on the type of design you have created, match plants to the landscape. Place grasses and ferns around a woodland pond, fill a quiet pool with water lilies and surround a marble fountain spraying water with delicate flowers.

Teakwood Garden Furniture by Barlow Tyrie

A wooden bench rests beside a quiet pond, through which goldfish swim beneath the lilies, and reeds at the edge wave in the breeze. The effect is a peaceful retreat where the water soothes, lulling its visitors to sleep.

Water flowing down this rocky stream bed enters the pool below with a splash. Although the scene could be taken from a mountain meadow, this stream is part of a larger domestic landscape.

Another bench beside another body of water creates a scene altogether different from the previous one. This landscape has a wakeful tone, with grasses, rocks and vines lying scattered throughout the area and wildlife possibly peering out from the grass. And although this scene, too, looks like it belongs in the wild, the fence behind attests to a human touch.

Hosta, creeping ivy, snapdragons and various other plants encircle this pool, climbing over rocks and shading its sides with their deep green leaves. The pool reflects the sky above and trees branching over its side. A small spray of water pours into the pool, helping to oxygenate the water.

Here, a tiny kidney-shaped pool housing lilies and goldfish peeks through flowers and grass like a liquid eye. Tiles and a cement bench border the pool, adding a touch of elegance.

185

SPECIAL FEATURES

Climate

Climate has a direct impact on your landscape. Factors such as sun, rain, snow, fog, wind, humidity and even city smog will affect your choice of trees, shrubs, plants and flowers. Research your area so you are familiar with the type of climate you live in, and peruse gardening books to determine which plants do best in your area.

Gardens do best when adapted to the climate. Remember that the number and length of seasons where you live will determine how much time you will be spending outside. Coastal regions can be either balmy and mild or windy and cold; southern states have longer growing seasons and plants easily survive their mild winters; places with lots of cold should consider hardier plants, trees and bushes as well as structures that look attractive bare of leaves and covered with snow.

This photo and opposite page (bottom left) courtesy of Terry Tempus, TCT Landscaping

Untrimmed grass and various other plants lie scattered throughout this garden in full summer bloom, growing together in a jumble of colors and uneven textures.

Summer sunlight bakes this deck, making it perfect for sunbathing or just relaxing. Pillows and a wicker chair with umbrella overhead create a comfortable resting place. Decks such as these are ideal for hot, sunny climates.

Rather than trying to grow lush fields in a dry climate, this landscape uses blue fescue, an ornamental grass that grows in tufts, planted around a rocky outcrop. Other native plants surround the grass and complete the desert scene.

Evergreens leave a carpet of needles watered by a sprinkler, an essential source of water in drier climates. Hardy trees such as these grow throughout the continent and are at home in a variety of landscapes.

SPECIAL FEATURES

Extra Elements

Extra features and unusual items add the finishing touch to a landscape. They include unique and unusual shapes, colors and groupings that make an interesting landscape extraordinary.

The pictures that follow display items with distinctive traits and characteristics that point to the individuality of the one who installed them and add an extra element of creativity to each scene.

This photo and opposite page (top) courtesy of California Redwood Association

This distinctive pagoda-like redwood structure is a major focal point and gives the rest of the garden an Oriental theme which is carried out in the plants, flowers and other elements.

An arched redwood bridge spans an empty stone drainage ditch used for run-off from the street beyond. The bridge and bed of impatiens next to it add beauty to a scene usually considered unattractive.

A bubbling fountain surrounded by pink geraniums adds a perfect touch to this small brick courtyard.

Photo courtesy of Bachman's Landscaping Service. Sue Hartley, photography.

Here an ordinary birdbath rests beneath a tree and inside a bed surrounded by geraniums and juniper. The bath and birds it attracts add flair to this small landscape.

Teakwood Garden Furniture by Barlow Tyrie

A wooden bench cleverly encircles this broad tree, creating a comfortable and attractive resting place beneath the tree's branches.

A fountain resting inside the curve of a combination stone retaining wall and walkway doubles as a birdbath and rises up grandly among a bed of pink begonias.

A simple birdhouse made of stones, with a copper roof and twigs for beams, blends form and function. The house will not only be a home for birds but will add personality to the scene.

191

LIST OF CONTRIBUTORS

We'd like to thank the following companies for providing the photographs used in this book:

Anderson Design Services, Ltd.
P.O. Box 5264
Minnetonka, MN 55343-2264
(612) 473-8387

Anchor Wall Systems
8309 Brooklyn Blvd.
Brooklyn Park, MN 55445
(800) 473-4452

Archadeck®
U.S. Structures, Inc.
2112 West Laburnum Avenue
Richmond, VA 23227
(800) 722-4668

Bachman's Landscaping Service
6010 Lyndale Avenue South
Minneapolis, MN 55419
(612) 861-7600

Barlow Tyrie Inc.
1263 Glen Ave., Suite 230
Moorestown, NJ 08057
(609) 273-7878

Caddcon Designs, Inc.
4701 O'Donnell Street
Baltimore, MD 21224
(800) 821-DECK

California Redwood Association
405 Enfrente Drive, Suite 200
Novato, CA 94949
(415) 382-0662

Milt Charno & Associates
611 North Mayfair Road
Wauwatosa, WI 53226
(414) 475-0881

Classic & Country Crafts
5100-1B Clayton Rd., Suite 291
Concord, CA 94521
(510) 672-4337

Kristine Distel & Associates Landscaping
1844 Glenwood Pkwy.
Golden Valley, MN 55422
(612) 751-0377

Doner Design, Inc.
2175 Beaver Valley Pike
New Providence, PA 17560
(717) 786-8891

Dundee Nursery & Landscape Company
16800 Hwy. 55
Plymouth, MN 55446
(612) 559-4004

Georgia-Pacific Corporation
133 Peachtree Street NE
P.O. Box 105605
Atlanta, GA 30348-5605
(404) 521-4000

Handcrafted Copper & Stone Sculpture
9796 West Bay Shore Drive
Traverse City, MI 49684
(616) 947-5259

Hanover Lantern
470 High Street
Hanover, PA 17331
(717) 632-6464

Holm & Olson
159 Duke Street
St. Paul, MN 55102
(612) 222-0521

Jackson & Perkins
Medford, OR 97501
(800) 854-6200

Kop-Coat, Inc.
Wolman® Protection
Products Division
Koppers Building K1824
Pittsburgh, PA 15219
(800) 556-7737

Lilypons Water Gardens
6800 Lilypons Road
P.O. Box 10
Buckeystown, MD 21717-0010
(800) 723-7667

Liteform Designs
P.O. Box 3316
Portland, OR 97208
(503) 257-8464

Kevin G. Norby & Associates, Inc.
10901 Red Circle Dr., Suite 125
Minnetonka, MN 55343
(612) 938-0020

Osmose Wood Preserving, Inc.
P.O. Drawer O
Griffin, GA 30224-0249
(800) 241-0240

P & M Cedar Products, Inc.
P.O. Box 7349
Stockton, CA 95267
(209) 957-6360

Southern Pine Marketing Council
P.O. Box 641700
Kenner, LA 70064-1700
(504) 443-4464

TCT Landscaping
P.O. Box 1218
Solvang, CA 93464
(805) 688-3741

Toro News Center
1401 W. 76th St., Suite 420
Minneapolis, MN 55423
You may contact Toro News Center for a free brochure.

Western Wood Products Association
Yeon Bldg., 522 SW 5th Ave.
Portland, OR 97204-2122
(503) 224-3930

Weyerhaeuser
P.O. Box 189
R.D. #2 Campbell Road
Titusville, PA 16354
(800) 723-1012